I0803414

INDIA HICKS

AN ENTERTAINING STORY

INDIA HICKS

AN ENTERTAINING STORY

Foreword by Brooke Shields

Lifestyle Photography by India Hicks and Brittan Goetz
Food Photography by David Loftus

RIZZOLI NEW YORK

New York · Paris · London · Milan

Dedicated to the tribe of smart, beautiful, hardworking women who helped create our community, and a lot of lovely parties, from 2014 to 2019

TABLE OF CONTENTS

FOREWORD

by Brooke Shields

India and I met in London almost two decades ago at a party celebrating my debut in the West End as Roxie Hart in *Chicago*, but it was during my first trip to Harbour Island in 2006 that I became truly enamored of her. A mutual friend told me to call her up. I hesitated because it felt a bit presumptuous, but my husband, daughters, and I were promptly invited for dinner that evening. India met us at the arched stone entrance of the property surrounded by palm trees. She was barefoot, wearing a long, flowing dress, hair loosely tied back and not a drop of makeup on her lightly bronzed face, hugging her dachshund, Banger. I was instantly seduced (and immediately wished I had packed differently).

We spent our entire trip learning all the things she loved about this paradise. I began daydreaming that I, too, could craft a table setting or throw a garden party or decorate a cake with the same chic yet accessible style. I took my fantasy a bit too far when, one day, over (a few) Goombay Smashes, I boldly volunteered to host a proper tea for India to celebrate the launch of her skin-care line. Well, it's one thing to imagine yourself a hostess of her stature and talent, and quite another to actually pull it off. But her face lit up, and I felt I had to follow through. I managed to channel as much of my inner India as possible, and though the clotted cream was a bit hard to spread, overall the event was a great success.

Then there was the time I spontaneously decided to spend my birthday in the Bahamas. India leapt into action. In less than two hours, she transformed her outdoor table into an elegant, jungle-themed oasis. I had brought her zebra-print scarves from a line I was designing. Only India would dare to cut and transform them into tablecloths, napkins, and napkin rings! Under the stars and lit only by candles, white china and silver flatware were placed precisely, and fresh pink and peach hibiscus flowers provided color. It was breathtaking.

To this day, I remain awed by her innovation and inspired by her endless energy as well as the joy she infuses into her beautiful world of design.

INTRODUCTION

My mother taught me to ride horses, water-ski, and play canasta, but she certainly could not be bothered with domestic trivialities like cooking. So, for the past fifteen years, Claire Williams has swept into our kitchen, fed the kids, packed the picnics, roasted the chickens, and tossed the salads. She has prepared lunch for eight and dinner for 168. Without Claire, we would all be really hungry. Fondly known as our Top Banana, she has kindly allowed me to include a few of her secret recipes here.

This book is really a series of entertaining stories—and hopefully you find them entertaining. There's one about my grandmother seated next to a cannibal king, another where my sister pees in an unplumbed loo, and one with goldfish swimming in Jell-O. There are also some helpful hints and simple suggestions, which now, with a few decades of experience, I can offer, like using your duvet cover as a tablecloth, teacups as vases, luggage labels as place cards, real roses on a fake cake, and a garage as a dining room.

Of course, I am aware that not all of us are able to set up a table on a pink-sand beach or have drinks at the end of a dock overlooking a tropical sunset, but perhaps these images will set your imagination alight or lead you to dream a little more.

Intimate, unpolished, and slightly haphazard: this is how I entertain.

OPPOSITE: The main ingredient to most of these entertaining stories is my family: David, my five children, my siblings, my mother, and Claire, who is seen here being hugged by Conrad on her wedding day, which we hosted at our home Hibiscus Hill.

LET'S START WITH A DRINK

Waitrose
HARVEYS
Coca-Cola
LEA & PERRINS
TABASCO

THE SIZE OF THE CUBE

Setting the scene

The start, or possibly the end, of a new friendship is always helped by a drink. It breaks the ice and sets the scene.

It was early evening on our terrace in the Bahamas. We were well into a second round of drinks with new friends. We had only recently met, and so we wanted to make them feel at home and, of course, leave a good impression. The wife left for a moment, slipping out to find the bathroom. Suddenly, a bloodcurdling scream was heard. We leapt up and rushed inside. There was the wife, standing on the threshold of the bathroom, nervously pointing. Inside, in the dark, tied up to a chair, was a smallish child. His feet and hands were desperately wriggling, bound by heavy ropes, and his three older brothers were suspiciously absent.

Now if your father happened to be a designer who designed everything around him, including the bowling alley of the White House and his own cape, lined in scarlet silk, you would not be surprised to learn that he also designed his own ice cubes. He went to great lengths to find very large oversize ice trays, which had a steel handle-thing you levered in order to release the very large oversize cubes, which were then placed in a sleek stainless-steel ice bucket. The size of the cube was everything.

My father was eccentric in many respects; he ate his strawberries covered in pepper, and he always let the fizz out of a Coca-Cola before drinking it. But don't for a minute think he drank it au naturel—it was heavily laced with alcohol. One of the few times my mother ever lost her temper with him, she happened to be drinking Coca-Cola, not laced and with its fizz. She became so exasperated that she threw her glass across the room, resulting in a wall covered by the drink. "Brilliant!" said my father, and thereafter he made a career out of painting rooms a dark, shiny Coca-Cola color. About the only drink I never saw my father touch was Pimm's. I, on the other hand, am happy to drink this taste of summer even at Christmas.

OPPOSITE: Pimm's, the archetypal English drink and the star of the Henley Royal Regatta, Wimbledon, and our own bar. FOLLOWING PAGES, LEFT: Simple tiny gestures like carnation buds, even bought in a rush, snipped down, and arranged quickly, just add a bit more to those important drinking moments. They don't even have to be in vases—I have used discarded fragrance bottles and old olive-oil jars. FOLLOWING PAGES, RIGHT: David Hicks–sized ice cubes. He would never stand for those ridiculous half moon–shaped ones that come pouring out of a machine. PAGE 18: Me, testing the theory that you can have a quiet drink anywhere. PAGE 19: With two glasses, a bottle of champagne, and a pitcher of roses, no one is going to care if you are at the end of a dock or in the kitchen at home. Keep romance alive, dudes.

THE CULINARY IDIOT

Even I can produce a platter

How much you like your guests coming over for drinks depends on how far you go. Perhaps a troublesome neighbor is not offered even a peanut, but a potential investor or a new mother-in-law needs some seducing. It seems that trays and platters laden with edible displays are on-trend for a reason. First, even an unskilled culinary idiot like me can gather together some inventive ingredients and lay them out temptingly; think black rice sticks or local honeycomb, exotic dates and fruity salami, seasonable figs and stinky cheeses. And second, with all this choice, we can navigate the increasing and confusing dietary requirements of the modern man and woman.

We are blessed to live between the Bahamas and Britain, and we take full advantage of those climates. We have drinks by a roaring fire on a Sunday morning in England or drinks on a floating dock in the Bahamas in the evening. If a floating dock is not available, I would encourage you to still think imaginatively about where you could possibly have a few friends over for a drink: a tree house in the garden, under the shade of a shed in the yard, or around an unusual table inside the home.

We once had Mick Jagger round for a drink, oh you know, as you do. We didn't really know each other. In fact, when he called the first time after a friend put us in touch, my other half, David, answered the phone, said "Hello," and heard a raspy, vaguely familiar voice. "Who is this?" said David. "It's Mick Jagger," said Mick Jagger. "Very funny," said David, and he hung up, knowing it was a prank. There was a terrible storm when Mick and his kid came over, so we ended up cross-legged on the floor around a short table in our sitting room, drinking and playing Jenga and eating from a platter of random delights I had managed to pull together.

OPPOSITE: Surely there must be enough choice here to navigate the increasing and confusing dietary requirements of the modern man and woman. If you can't find something on this platter to munch on, I give up.

ONE DROP
RUM

THE MARQUESS'S BANANA DAIQUIRI

As told by David Flint Wood

On our way back from the Out Islands, my oldest friend and I used to stop at the Traveller's Rest tavern on West Bay Street in Nassau, where we would drink banana daiquiris and play Connect 4 while waiting for the plane to London. We recently reconvened in our own sort of re-tox retreat and sought to re-create these memories....

1. Fill a blender with ice.
2. Add:
   Juice of 1 whole Persian lime or 3 key limes
   1 tbsp. brown sugar
   2–3 bananas (depending on how banana-y you feel)
   Generous amount of golden rum,* and then some more
3. Blend until the ice is crushed.
4. Begin Connect 4 (optional).

OPPOSITE, CLOCKWISE FROM TOP LEFT: Celebrating the cycle of life should include a good bottle of locally made rum. A homemade wreath in the spirit of summer. A fresh daiquiri with a spoonful of sugar to make the medicine go down. Homegrown sugar bananas. FOLLOWING PAGE, LEFT: The only trouble with a tree-house location for drinks is coming back down to earth afterward. FOLLOWING PAGE, RIGHT: David tells me this is not a Bloody Mary, this is a Bullish Caesar—whatever that is.

LEA
&
PERRINS
WORCESTERSHIRE
TABASCO

Missing Woman Intensifies
The New York
York City

DAVID'S BULLISH CAESAR

As told by David Flint Wood

Tomato juice is rather too thick for the tropics—only the Italians know how to make thin tomato juice—so I use Clamato, but since not everyone is wholly reconciled with the thought of clam juice, I split it with beef broth. (The slightly lighter version produced by Swanson's is better in the heat than the Campbell's dark version.) In this way, I also like to think that my noonday prescription represents virtually every food group known to dietitians—more even than the "daily five," if you're counting.

1. Fill a cocktail shaker with ice.
2. Add:
   - 2 jiggers of Tabasco
   - 2 jiggers of Lea & Perrins Worcestershire Sauce
   - Juice of 1 whole lemon
   - ¼ bottle cap of sherry
   - 2 fingers of vodka (I use Stolichnaya—what's good enough for Connery is good enough for me)
3. Fill the rest of the shaker's available space with an equal share of beef broth and Clamato juice.
4. Shake vigorously and serve over ice with a stick of celery. If you have any energy left, add a pinch of celery salt.

OPPOSITE: David on a Sunday winter morning in Bellport, New York, having been force-marched down a frozen beach in boots and gloves. A new and rather alarming experience for him.

OPPOSITE AND ABOVE: Entertaining often involves drinking. Drinking can involve wine. Lots of wine leaves one with lots of crates. In the past, we used the leftover wine crates as steps for small children to reach the sink when brushing their small teeth. Now we use them as a way to host a mass of wildflowers. Piled beneath the flowers is a heap of wet newspaper, poofing the display up and giving the stems a drink of their own.

CHEAT WITH SUSHI

There's no time for perfect

It's hard to say what creates the perfect drinks hour. Interesting guests, stylish hors d'oeuvres, perfectly polished children singing "Edelweiss"? In reality, who has the time to make it perfect, especially since most of us haven't slept since 1997. So cheat. For God's sake, cheat. Invite friends who bring their own martinis, negotiate with a teenager to make sure the speaker is charged and the candles lit, and order in some chilled sushi bites. But make damn sure the fridge is working first.

Living on an island prone to long power outages and electrical surges has its challenges. After one such attack, we were left with a fridge that gave anyone who dared touch it an electrical shock. It was mild at first, a gentle buzzing that would travel down your arm, but increasingly over time it became a head-to-toe, hair-on-end sort of shock.

We don't live on the kind of island where you pop out and buy a new fridge. We live on the kind of island where you order a fridge from another country, wait for it to be trucked to a port, have it loaded into a container and onto a boat, travel across an ocean, be unloaded in the Bahamas, mortgage your home to pay for the duty, have it released from customs, hunt down a vehicle large enough to drive it up to your house, find strong arms to carry it in, and then wait for days, possibly weeks, till the one electrician servicing the whole community can find the time to wire it in.

But you learn to adapt, so even the eleven-year-old knows that the man-sized pair of rubber flip-flops now permanently in front of the fridge are there for a reason. You slip them on before opening the door. Just for everyday survival.

Meanwhile, you've invited friends over for a drink who think they will be helpful in taking out the chilled sushi, and you all shout "Noooooo!" as you see their innocent hand take hold of the fridge handle, not understanding the shock they are about to receive.

OPPOSITE: Divine sushi from Da Vine. If you stumble upon Harbour Island, be sure to nip in here—they treat sushi as an art form.

DAVE'S FAMOUS MARTINI

As told by Dave Stewart of the Eurythmics

I have always been obsessed with rituals. When I was a young boy, I had to polish my boots with Kiwi black polish and a soft brush, moving round the boot from right to left whilst kneeling in front of my football uniform, which was laid out as if I were already in it. This could not be interrupted in any way or there would be hell to pay, and my parents knew this. It's the same when I'm planning a concert: every detail has to be attended to right up to the stage entrance—entrances are so important, as are exits. The perfect martini is beholden to its own rituals: for example, when to have one (around 7:44 p.m., before dinner) and when not to have one (after dinner, or after 10 p.m.). I always have a notebook handy, as I know exactly halfway through this magic elixir, the left side of my brain starts to pull up the tent pegs and decamp whilst the right side begins to act like a dog let off its lead in the park, hurtling toward unknown territories full of ideas or melodies that must be written down, as I'm bound to have forgotten them once the second half of the martini is downed. I believe every melody is stuck somewhere among your thoughts, and a good old martini massages your brain enough to let these ideas escape and run free. The left side of your brain is always watching over you like the general of a lame and logical army, looking for signs of weirdness that may upset the applecart. Me, I like going creatively loco after a hard day's work, if you can call turning reality into dreams "work." Yes, that's my job, and it's all I know how to do—except make a bloody good martini.

1. Place 3 olives on a skewer into a martini glass.
2. Pour the tiniest splash of vermouth over the olives.
3. Take the vodka from the freezer (yep, the freezer).
4. Take ice cubes from the freezer and quickly fill a shaker halfway with ice.
5. As soon as you can, pour the vodka into the shaker and quickly start shaking. You want to prevent the ice from melting, which adds water, a terrible sin. (For the same reason, never put the glass in the freezer; water condenses on the frozen glass when it hits the air.)
6. Holding the olive skewer tight, swill the vermouth around the glass and then into the sink, leaving only a fine film inside the glass.
7. Pour the contents of the shaker on top of the olives, stopping half an inch before the top; you should see a few tiny fractals of ice on the surface of the slightly viscous vodka.
8. Clink glasses with a friend and sip immediately. Be prepared to go down the rabbit hole.

OPPOSITE: Dave Stewart's hands make memorable martinis as well as music.

THE UNEXPECTED

On being prepared

In life, we must be sure to expect the unexpected. Cocktail hour is no different.

It was the first time my cousin Tim was introducing his new bride, Isabella, to an older family friend of his parents. On arrival, they were shown into the drawing room and invited to sit around a small card table, where drinks were served. Before long, Isabella felt Tim's foot on her ankle, rubbing softly up and down. She became uneasy. This was not the time for footsie. She tried to kick him off. He ignored her, rubbing harder. She could feel herself blushing. The elderly hostess looked at her quizzically just as the door opened and the butler swept in. "Your Ladyship," he said. "It's Snoopy's suppertime." "Oh, how rude of me," said the hostess, turning again to Isabella. "I have not introduced Snoopy!" With that, she lifted the heavy fringed-velvet tablecloth to reveal a fat dachshund frantically humping Isabella's leg. "Ah," she said, "I see you have already met."

Just after my eighteenth birthday, I moved to Paris. I was terribly unconfident and uncultured. My older sister—who had taken Paris by storm a few years earlier—came to visit me with the intention of helping me settle into this sophisticated city. One evening, we were invited for a drink by a fashion photographer who had an apartment overlooking the Eiffel Tower. He had recently moved in; the smell of fresh paint lingered. After the first bottle of very rich French wine, the photographer went to open another and my sister went off to find the loo. When she reappeared, she whispered, "We have to leave now!" The loo she had peed in was simply being stored in his newly carpeted dressing room. It was not plumbed in. We left quickly. The second bottle of wine was never offered nor opened.

OPPOSITE: David had asked what I wanted for my birthday. I don't think he thought I was serious about a table made out of sand, but he built it nonetheless. I love the unexpected.

SUPER BLOW POP
mentos

A high-ranking general was invited to stay with my grandparents during the Second World War. My grandfather at the time was Chief of Combined Operations, and the general's visit was an important one. My grandmother, recently returned from a trip to Africa, had brought back with her a lion cub. Since arriving in England, the cub had grown significantly and was by now sporting an impressive mane and even more impressive teeth. The lion had padded innocently into the guest bathroom where the general was about to step out of the bath. Terrified, he promptly got back into the bath, remaining there shivering in fear until my grandmother sent someone upstairs to find out what was taking him so long to join them for a predinner drink.

The unexpected cannot always be avoided—humping dachshunds, unplumbed loos, terrified generals—but they make for interesting stories over a drink or two.

OPPOSITE: Unexpected also might be the offering of green lollipops and orange Cheetos along with asparagus tips and red pepper slices mingled together. Those are my kind of hors d'oeuvres, and every bored child who is dragged along by their parents admires my taste. The parents not so much. FOLLOWING PAGES, LEFT: A slice of lemon, a spring of rosemary, and a mint leaf jolly up any nonalcoholic offering. FOLLOWING PAGES, RIGHT: I wrapped patterned napkins around the seat cushions to give them a quick makeover. If only we could do this to ourselves.

OPPOSITE: Check your tide charts. One moment, it's the ultimate spot for a cocktail or two, and the next, your skirt is damp.
ABOVE: Lifeboat to the rescue.

WINNER, WINNER, CHICKEN DINNER

COMPANY'S COMING

Clean up fast

Especially if it's cousins. Or any family member, for that matter. They always make me nervous, perhaps because I was the youngest of ten very close cousins and siblings from two very close sisters. I had a lot to live up to. So when a family event is on the horizon, I go into sizzling overdrive. Not just the normal scampering-around-shoving-stuff-into-cupboards overdrive, but the hand-painting-invitations-while-pressing-your-great-grandfather's-embroidered-napkins kind of overdrive. Add in a touch of polishing the silver (none of it matches, but I think that's OK) and picking wildflowers from the garden, with a few bought in panic from the supermarket, slotted in, and hopefully undetected in the assembled arrangements.

Just after my mother's sister—my beloved aunt Patricia—died, I invited said cousins and siblings for a dinner so my mother could feel the warmth of her family still around her. Except it wasn't warm, it was bloody freezing. It was England. I thought we would be too squashed in our kitchen and had the bright idea of setting up in the garage. It did not take long to drive out the cars, sweep up the dust, unfold the stored tables and chairs, use a long stretch of fabric that was originally intended to re-cover a sofa as a tablecloth, and even hang a spare painting on an oak beam. Candles, piles of logs, a few firepits, and a view out to the golden wheat field set the scene, I thought. In fact, the last of the summer slipped away just as the candles were lit. Sun turned to rain and a wind whipped up around us, whooshing up not only the neatly folded napkins and the ladies' dresses, but also my mother's immaculate Elnett-ed hair. But actually, in that damp garage on that shivery evening, it was the words spoken and the memories revisited between cousins and siblings that mattered, not the bread rolls blowing off the table.

OPPOSITE: The more blown the roses, the prettier in my opinion. Especially when they are mingling with lavender and baby thistles in old jam jars. No pretensions here.

OPPOSITE: My mother's cutlery mingles with my father's. ABOVE: Summer just turning to autumn, which could lead to an unexpected chilly evening, where dinner in an open garage is not such a good idea after all. FOLLOWING PAGES: It takes a long time for my mother's hair to be backcombed into such perfection, and about as long to wrap string and leaves around candles in the mad idea that this generates a happy atmosphere for the family gathering. What actually fosters the atmosphere is staying off politics, parenting, and religion.

CHICKEN POTPIE

Serves 4

Ingredients

4 whole boneless skinless chicken breasts
1 bay leaf
10 black peppercorns
5½ cups (1.3 L) chicken broth
6 tbsp. (85 g) salted butter, divided
1 lb. (453 g) leeks, cleaned and thinly sliced
8 oz. (227 g) white button mushrooms, thinly sliced
Salt and pepper
¼ cup (56 g) all-purpose flour
½ lb. (227 g) puff-pastry dough (homemade or store-bought)
1 egg, beaten

Directions

1. Preheat oven to 390°F (200°C).
2. Add chicken breasts, bay leaf, black peppercorns, and broth to a saucepan and poach gently until the chicken is just cooked.
3. Remove the chicken and discard the bay leaf and peppercorns, but reserve the broth. Shred the chicken into bite-size pieces. Melt 2 tbsp. (28 g) butter in a skillet on medium heat, then add the leeks and cover skillet with a tight-fitting lid to sweat them. Sweat until soft but not brown, about 15 minutes. Remove lid and add the mushrooms and cook for another 5 minutes. Mix the shredded chicken with the leeks and mushrooms. Season with salt and pepper.
4. In a saucepan, melt the remaining butter, add the flour, and cook on medium for 2 minutes or until well combined. Take the pan off the heat and add the reserved chicken broth. Return pan to the heat and keep stirring until you have a smooth sauce that is just bubbling. Add the sauce to the chicken mixture and combine, then pour mixture into a 9-inch pie dish or 4 individual ovenproof dishes.
5. Roll out puff-pastry dough and cut it big enough to fit on top of your dish or dishes. Dampen the edges of the dish with water and lay the pastry lid on top and press down slightly. Use any leftover dough to decorate the pie.
6. Make two vents in the middle of the dough and brush entire top with the beaten egg.
7. Bake for about 25 minutes, or until the pastry is golden brown.

OPPOSITE: Top Banana's traditional homemade potpie, embellished with fancy-looking leaves and eaten on our laps in front of the telly. Not so fancy. FOLLOWING PAGES, LEFT: After Eights in our family are not really for eating, they are for the After Eight game. Place said chocolate on the top of your forehead, and wiggle your face till the chocolate reaches your mouth. If you use your hands or the chocolate drops to the floor, you obviously won't be invited back. FOLLOWING PAGES, RIGHT: If you can find the time or someone with a tiny bit of talent to hand-draw an invitation, do so. It makes all the difference.

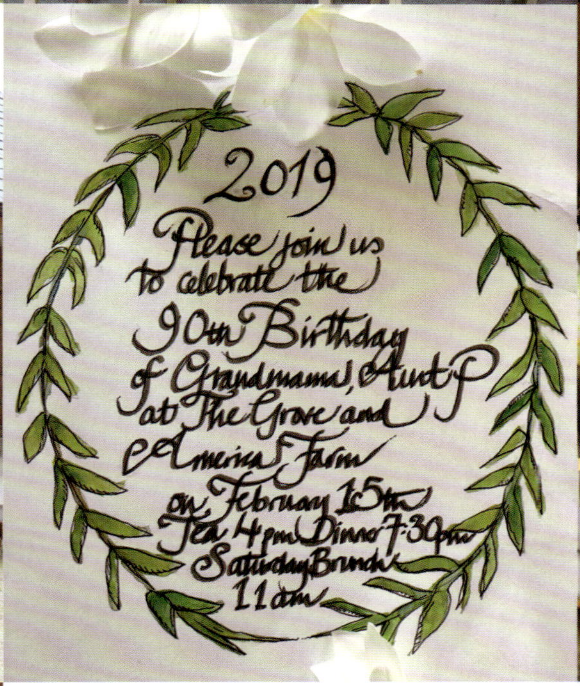
2019
Please join us
to celebrate the
90th Birthday
of Grandmama, Aunt P
at The Grove and
America Farm
on February 15th
Tea 4pm Dinner 7:30pm
Saturday Brunch
11am

A SLICE OF ENGLAND

Beating the weather odds

Having learned from the windy garage experience the next time I hosted a dinner, I really wanted it to be a winner, winner, chicken dinner and decided to invest in a minuscule Chinese hat marquee, so called because it was pointy on the top. This turned out to be the best investment I could have made, and incidentally I have used this party trick several times since. I sourced it locally and inexpensively, and a couple of burly men roll it out and put it up in no time. The sides can be left open in summer or closed in winter, and inside it cozily fits forty or so best friends. (I don't actually have forty best friends. I have to bribe people to come with the offer of a free book or something.)

And when my last book launched I did exactly that, wrapping up copies with a soft gray grosgrain ribbon and inviting friends for dinner and a small slice of England. We drank Pimm's in the garden surrounded by the smell of cow parsley and honeysuckle, which the bees were enjoying. Vases of roses hung from the trees, and guests wandered barefoot across the freshly mown lawn. Some years ago David fell in love with this bare-breasted plaster-cast bust. I did not. On this evening, I startled David by placing her on the drinks table. "I thought you did not even like her," he said. "I don't, but she might as well enjoy the evening with the rest of us," I replied. I think adding a surprise element to any evening makes it all the more memorable, except when it comes to chocolate soufflés for starters.

My mother, like me, is not comfortable in the kitchen, so she would be rescued by a Bahamian cook while holidaying each year in the Bahamas. One year, my mother came armed with a recipe for a hot chocolate soufflé. It was a new challenge for the cook, but one she seemed confident she could tackle. Just as we sat down to begin dinner, the kitchen door was thrown open and out walked the cook, triumphantly carrying a perfectly risen chocolate soufflé. My mother had forgotten to explain that chocolate soufflés were served at the end of the meal, not at the beginning.

OPPOSITE: Key ingredients for a successful evening: wildflowers, ribaldry, wine, and attentive ladies.
FOLLOWING PAGES: At the end of the lane in the garden of a deserted old farm grew a mass of roses, honeysuckle, and cow parsley. With Wellie boots on feet, I slipped under the gate and snipped away with my secateurs—the colors were not quite what I would have chosen, pinks and slightly sickly purples, but free is free.

ICEBREAKERS

Sparking conversation

Sparking conversation between guests can be more challenging than getting that soufflé to rise. I try to stir up our dinners by mixing up the location and the menus, but also the guests themselves. Occasionally it's a risk, so now I stack the guest list with someone I know who has an interesting story to tell, like Captain Bob. When prompted, he will keep our friends spellbound with his tales of being struck by lightning, fired at by pirates (he was a fisherman crewing ships with valuable lobster cargoes), and bitten by a shark. You can guess who won that fight. My great-grandmother, a remarkable woman who traveled the world, once sat next to the last of the cannibal kings at a formal dinner. She could not resist asking him what human flesh tasted like. Without hesitation, he replied, "Babies' fingers are simply delicious."

If you don't have a Captain Bob or a cannibal king to spark conversation, perhaps enlist one of your young-adult children. Amory, one of mine, was once seated at dinner between a husband and wife, neither of whom he had previously met, but both of whom he was able to captivate with a bit of mischief. The husband, to his left, asked him what he was doing with his life. "Oh, I am studying at a university for the creative arts," he said. "I want to be a filmmaker—or, rather, an auteur." A little while later the wife, on his other side, turned to him and also asked what he was doing with his life. "Oh, I am learning how to bake cinnamon rolls. I want to become a world-class baker and reignite the cinnamon bun." Can you imagine the conversation between the husband and wife when they were driving home after dinner?

OPPOSITE: When we can't fit everyone inside, we move outside. Down the driveway, on the top of our little hill, around our terrace, or even through the palm avenue. Folding tables and chairs are light and easy to put up and take down, and this is when having five kids with ten hands finally makes sense. FOLLOWING PAGES, LEFT: Island life often means we don't have the resources we would like at hand. There is no nipping out to Target. We repurpose, borrow, and upcycle as much as possible. Here, not having vases at the height I wanted, I turned the existing shorter vases upside down and balanced the flowers and candles on top to create elevation. FOLLOWING PAGES, RIGHT: When asked what my favorite gift has been, I say several reels of Festoon LED unbreakable lights. They were an unusual but genius hostess gift from a generous, imaginative friend.

CUCUMBER, FETA, AND PISTACHIO SALAD

Serves 6

Ingredients

A good amount of any lettuce of your choice

Two large cucumbers, thinly sliced with a potato peeler, a vegetable peeler, or a mandoline

Half a red onion, thinly sliced

2 medium ripe avocados, or 1 large, sliced

6 oz. (170 g) of feta cheese, diced

A good handful of shelled pistachio nuts

Juice of 1 lemon

Good olive oil

Salt and pepper

Directions

1. Put the lettuce into the bottom of your salad bowl.
2. On top of the lettuce, arrange your cucumbers, red onion, avocado, and feta cheese. Sprinkle on the pistachio nuts.
3. Pour on the lemon juice, then a couple of good glugs of the olive oil. Season with salt and pepper, and you're ready to go.

OPPOSITE: Twenty-five years ago, when David and I moved to Harbour Island, you could not find such luxuries as feta cheese or pistachio nuts. You could barely find toothpaste. You could, however, find fresh avocados grown locally, but we would not have dreamt of spreading them on toast or mixing in a smoothie or salad. FOLLOWING PAGES: David and I removed as much of the cement and glass in our home as possible and introduced softer, more natural elements like wood and rattan. We also try to tablescape with more natural textures and fabrics. By the way, my father claimed to have invented the word *tablescape*. Like a well-tailored coat, a nice set of white plates is a worthy investment: they will never go out of fashion, and they will last a lifetime.

POTATO DAUPHINOISE
India Hicks
David Flint Wood

David Flint Wood

India
David F.W.

Scarlett
Cole

Tom
Geordie
Chris

Hibiscus Hill
Suzanne
Summer 2019

Jeanette
India
Friday, September 25, 2015
Lunch & Lecture featuring
India Hicks
Arugula and Bibb Lettuce Salad with Hearts of
Palm, Cucumber, Tomatoes and Green Lentils with
Grilled Chicken and Cane Syrup Vinaigrette
Springerle Cookies by
Matt Edwards Fine Foods
Sponsored by

Martina
Elizabeth
Rea
Tom

Walker

PLACEMENT

More commonly known as a seating plan

Can you remember how it felt being picked last for the sports team? Just standing, waiting awkwardly as everyone else was chosen? I get that slightly sickly feeling when I go to a dinner and realize the seating is freestyle, wondering if I can get away with sitting next to David or saving a seat for the only other friend I might find there. Of course, neither are acceptable. At all. You only get to sit next to your other half during the time you are engaged. After that, it's a no-no. I sigh in relief when I spy a placement (pronounced the French way, with a slow, exaggerated emphasis on each syllable: plaaacement), spot place cards, or am directed by a helpful hostess to the chair she has designated for me.

So when it comes to my own dinners, yessss, I like to have a seating plan to ensure no one ever feels like he or she is standing on the edge of that sports field waiting and waiting. Traditionally you will place the most important woman on the right of the host and vice versa, with the most important man on the hostess's right, but I like to keep things as informal as possible and will often swap seats with another guest after the main course, so that formal-hierarchy nonsense gets a bit more smoothed over. Unless, that is, I see neighbors deep in a riveting conversation or old friends reconnecting or guests simply enjoying one another's company. Then I leave the whole damn thing alone, because it's working.

Once when we had Lenny Kravitz come over for supper, we ate in the kitchen—no formalities, no seating plan—but I wondered afterward if it might have helped my mother for there to have been a place card with his name on it. "Who was that nice man?" she asked. "Was I right in hearing his name was Zinny Crayfish?" It got even weirder when Lenny wandered into the TV room to find my boys playing Guitar Hero, which was the hot new commodity. "Can I have a go?" asked Lenny, picking up a plastic guitar and starting to strum. Felix, then aged around ten, pointed out to Lenny that he was actually one of the computerized "heroes" on the screen. Lenny was playing Lenny.

OPPOSITE: I have an overstock of postcards, luggage labels, and pebbles from the beach, so our place cards can be fairly bonkers. They're normally written on my hands and knees, but sometimes they're taken more seriously and calligraphed by a professional, or a daughter with a pinch of glitter and a secret message inside.

SEEING RED

I like a bit of a theme

My brother accuses me of going all "Gracious Home" when I entertain, and that's not a compliment. Celebrating the full moon one month, when lots of friends were visiting the island, was an excuse for a big, long dinner table covered in flame-tree branches. The best bit about decorating with flame-tree branches is that they are free. At a certain time of year, this tree bursts into bloom all over the island. I stand on my tiptoes on the roof of our Jeep and cut down ripe limbs. With a lot of fishing line and some extra hands, I cover balustrades, steps, and tabletops. At one point I stand back and think it's marvelous, and then I stand back farther and think it's all been a mistake—this looks like a Hawaiian wedding. At other times of year, I use whatever else might be in bloom in the Bahamas: sugar apples and mangoes, pineapples and sweet bananas. If I am in the English countryside, I might use blackberry branches and roses or artichokes and thistles. I try to improvise and be nimble in my thinking, although it's not always a success or appreciated. "What is this horrible brown cloth?" David asked when seeing the full-moon table laid out.

OPPOSITE: Considering Skunk was found as an abandoned, starving kitten, she has acquired considerable airs and graces.

ABOVE: Sometimes new ideas are a success, and sometimes not. This felt more like a Hawaiian wedding than a full-moon party. I would not repeat a brown tablecloth again, but it had been donated as a freebie by a friend, so I was seduced into the idea. The flame-tree branches are a freebie from Mother Nature. She is always generous.

ABOVE: Dressing to match your decor is not always a clever practice. You might be mistaken for a tablecloth.

ABOVE: Experimenting again with the orange flame-tree flowers. This was more successful without the poop-brown tablecloth. OPPOSITE: Peas on toast, lanterns on stairs, a thumbs-up from Conrad, and a ridiculous time-consuming attempt at an original watermelon punch bowl that will not be repeated. FOLLOWING PAGES, LEFT: Wrestling with Bond. And one of the few times we kept our table clinically clean—only hurricane lamps and candles. FOLLOWING PAGES, RIGHT: I can barely boil an egg. But I can stabilize a candle in pink sand.

ABOVE: Mangoes and sugar apples were evidently in season.

ABOVE: The day after this dinner, the little community school was awash with fruit. FOLLOWING PAGES, LEFT: A few surprised tourists wandering up from the beach came across our table laid up in the sandy lane. From this spot, we could catch the sun setting. FOLLOWING PAGES, RIGHT: David's homegrown bananas, with their exotic and slightly creepy tentacle, and some asparagus, sugar apples, and genips, a Bahamian fruit that could be likened to a lychee and is a great treat when stolen from someone's tree.

THE MISSING KING

And fish waits for no one

My mother is vaguely related to the Spanish royal family, and the Greek, and at one time the Romanovs, and definitely the Swedes. Lots of royal families thought it was sensible to marry into one another's families, keeping monarchies strong and safe. Now they've had another idea: marrying perfectly normal people.

Anyway, when a wandering king of Spain sails through the islands, we'll offer him a hot meal. We set a date and a time and starch and re-starch the white tablecloths. I brought out all the blue-and-white china and it felt vaguely regal, despite having been discovered in a secondhand shop in our little local town of Wallingford in England. The plates did not quite match and were, I think, not just second- but possibly fourth-hand. We removed a snoozing cat from the large blue-and-white bowls, filled them with water, floated tea lights and frangipani flowers, and lit the candlesticks that David had bought me for Christmas one year and waited for the royal arrival. And waited. And waited.

Other friends had arrived, and we all decided to enjoy a drink whilst waiting. Top Banana was growing anxious in the kitchen; her fish did not wait for anyone. We decided to have another drink. I dispatched a few of my boys to the harbor to see if they could hunt down the missing king. Whilst pouring another glass of wine, I e-mailed and texted, trying to reach him. It was then that David had the rather brilliant old-fashioned idea of picking up the phone and calling. "Ah, India, my dear!" said a voice on the other end. "We are so looking forward to your dinner next week." I hung up and poured myself another glass of wine, and Claire served the fish, which was cooked to perfection.

OPPOSITE: Fish fit for a king. Obviously.

OPPOSITE: Preparing for dinner can be exhausting. Gloria agrees. ABOVE: Bamboo candlesticks, a non-anniversary present from David. Because we don't have an anniversary.

ABOVE: I discovered these plates in a dusty antiques shop in England. There were only a few in each pattern, and I was hopelessly unable to make up a complete set. I loved them all the more for that. And the price of them was around a dollar a plate. OPPOSITE: If the bowls are not occupied with sleeping cats, we'll fill them with oranges or shells or coconuts. Or water and floating candles and petals.

APPLE AND BLACKBERRY CRUMBLE

Serves 8

Ingredients

6 cups (about 1½ lbs. or 680 g) peeled, cored, and sliced Bramley or other sharp apples

⅓ cup packed brown sugar

1 tbsp. lemon juice

1 cup fresh blackberries

1¼ cups all-purpose flour

6 tbsp. (84 g) cold unsalted butter, cut into small pieces

½ cup granulated sugar

Directions

1. Preheat oven to 375°F (190°C). Add apples, brown sugar, lemon juice, and blackberries to a bowl and mix well. Pour mixture into an 8- or 9-inch round ovenproof pie dish.
2. Sift flour into a mixing bowl and cut in the butter with a pastry blender, two knives, or your fingers until the mixture resembles a coarse meal.
3. Add the granulated sugar to the flour mixture and stir well to combine.
4. Sprinkle the flour mixture over the filled pie dish.
5. Bake in the oven for about 30 minutes, or until bubbling.

OPPOSITE: This basket has been used by many generations. As a child, my mother would have it in hand when blackberry picking, and then me, and now Domino.

THE BLUES

Careful and crafty

Actually, this was the exact opposite of the blues. This was a hugely joyful dinner that we set up in Los Angeles. I still had my company and a very strong community of women who stood beside each other, supporting one another. This was an evening where we thanked our lucky stars for all that the business had brought us, although it had not brought us quite enough to not be under a strict budget. We just had to be careful and crafty.

Needing a gift for each of the girls who came, I did a little warehouse research and learned that we had a slight overstock of towels—enough as a gift for all. And then it dawned on me: why not snip and sew the other remaining towels into a table runner?

I found the paper lanterns on Amazon, bought the bamboo sticks at a wholesale outlet place, and tied them together with fishing line. I worked with a superb and sympathetic event organizer who trimmed down her team and found us not only a location, but also the chairs and cutlery that were a fairly crucial part of the dinner. She shared one good secret with me, which was "Guests of guests cannot bring guests," a.k.a. be strict about my invite list and I might meet my budget. And I shared one good secret with her, which was to sew coins into tablecloth corners to stop them blowing about in a California breeze.

I persuaded a dear and talented friend to compose and sing a musical toast, the first verse of which went like this:

> *At first it sounded bonkers!*
> *But a notion worth a try—*
> *An upscale revolution*
> *In the way smart women buy;*
> *A thrilling, wild adventure,*
> *An amazing coup de grâce!*
> *Never underestimate the power*
> *Of ladies who kick ass!*

He was certainly right in one respect: it was a thrilling, wild adventure.

OPPOSITE: Beach towels as table runners. I think this counts as shopping your closet.

WHAT'S FOR LUNCH?

DEALT LEMONS?

Give a lunch

Two things happen when you live in the tropics: you eat outside a lot, and you get fooled into believing you should be growing your own lemons. (OK, other things happen, too, like sunburn and snakes.)

Sometimes all of these things happen at once. Amy and Aerin were coming for lunch, two women in the design world who need little introduction if you follow beauty or interiors. First time to the island, first time to our house. It was spring-break time, so there was a flock of kids, too. We are always able to quickly enlarge any table by adding an enormous piece of plywood on top and dressing it up with a tablecloth. This also gives us more space on the table for a bit of decorating drama. On this occasion, though, drama came from elsewhere. Imagine the scene: we are in our sitting room having a prelunch drink, a hummingbird is feeding on the nectar of the bright pink bougainvillea tree growing on the terrace, Banger is lying under the fan on his back, even my children are vaguely calm. We go through to lunch, and there are satisfactory oohs and aahs as the guests smell the fragrance of the lemons mingling with the wild vines and frangipani petals that I had arranged down the table. Aerin reaches to pull out the chair I've suggested she sit in and lets out a screech. There, coiled all around the chairback, is a long, long snake, snoozing in the afternoon sun.

We had become rather familiar with the snake as he, or a relative, had recently slithered between the tiny bars of our birdcage (sold to us as completely snake-proof). Once inside, the snake had eaten one of our lovebirds and then had the audacity to fall asleep, overstuffed from his lunch, inside the cozy wooden nesting box, whilst the other little lovebirds sat shivering in fear, wondering who would be next.

OPPOSITE: Over the years, we have amassed quite a throng of serving trays, platters, and baskets. Whether entertaining in a city, beside a mountain, or on a beach, I like the warmth that the natural texture of wicker, seagrass, raffia, and sisal bring. And it's super easy to line them with a napkin for a little zhuzh. FOLLOWING PAGES, LEFT: A lunch setup showing that it's OK to bring your fancy dining room chairs outside every so often, add a gigantic piece of plywood on top of the table for additional legroom, and stick to the drama of a good centerpiece rather than an uninvited snake snoozing in the sunshine. FOLLOWING PAGES, RIGHT: Lemon chicken. Carrying the theme a bit too far?

Cream
of The
Crop

WHO SITS WHERE

Be done with hierarchy

Even at lunches when we tempt newer friends to join us, we'll have thought out who sits where. At big business lunches, government dinners, and charity balls, strict seating codes still apply. In India during the time my grandparents were there as viceroy and vicereine, the seating placement was done by hierarchy of the province or state you were from. For example, if you were the governor of Bombay—a vast province—at a governor's conference, you would be the chief guest and placed in the numero uno spot; if you were governor of a smaller province, you would be more modestly placed. The only problem with this in a country such as India is that you might be seated next to someone who did not speak the same dialect as you. So lunch would be had in unbearable silence. When Indira Gandhi came into power as prime minister of India, my mother remembers her saying how ridiculous this was, grading everyone by status and yet being unable to converse. She would be doing things differently, she said, making a seating plan designed so guests could actually talk to one another. A few weeks later, my mother asked her how this new arrangement had gone. "Disastrously!" she said. "The French ambassador stormed out, saying he had never been so insulted when seeing his seat all the way down the table."

There was a moment when we thought growing our own lemons at home in the Bahamas was a romantic idea. Native lemons are known as "scrubby lemons" because they have a bumpy, rough texture on the outside. We learned fairly soon that you can't just take a lemon pip and plant it, though. Well, you can, but the resulting lemons are extra sour and need a complicated grafting system in order to be edible. Turns out, life never gave us lemons—we, the human race, invented them all by ourselves.

OPPOSITE: The plates were designed by me and made from melamine, which means they are pretty much unbreakable. I hoped they looked like handcrafted porcelain plates from Florence. Instead of the illustrious words *In Honor Bound* on the family coat of arms, I added some ridiculous sayings for fun. The words here read *Cream of the Crop*, but we also had *I love chocolate*. However, because I am so dyslexic (and for a dyslexic, that's a hard word to spell), I misspelled *chocolate* and the plates went into production before anyone noticed.
FOLLOWING PAGES: A close friend felt we were lacking in color. He gave me this turquoise bowl from Greece and a bright yellow blanket from Nicaragua. Vincent, our tortoise, gives not a damn about color as long as his lunch is watermelon.

A TOUCH OF THE UNUSUAL

Goldfish and Jell-O

Because I am blessed with a Top Banana who does the cooking for us, I get more time to fiddle with knives and forks and the atmosphere in general. That's if I'm not trying to run a business. If I'm trying to run a business, which I did for six very frantic years, then all bets are off. But on any occasion, I encourage a touch of the unusual, whether it's inviting our tortoise to lunch, placing scarlet-red carnations in a pool-blue porcelain pot, or corralling some tiny tots for sandwiches inside our hexagonal playhouse.

My grandmother not only encouraged the unusual, she was also unusual herself. She traveled to many places in the world that no other Western woman had ever been before. She was wealthy and adventurous, which helped. On her travels, she tasted many exotic delicacies and experienced how others in faraway lands entertained. At home, she had an excellent French chef who once created an unusual dessert for a large lunch party of visiting friends: a bright orange Jell-O mold surrounding a glass bowl in which goldfish were swimming.

OPPOSITE: The white house. FOLLOWING PAGES, LEFT: If you're running a household, a business, and a kitchen, it might be worth not setting the table and instead simply stacking plates, fanning out napkins, and leaving guests to pick up their own knives and forks. FOLLOWING PAGES, RIGHT: Crudités in bowls and beer in tubs, with big ice blocks thrown in and a game of chess on standby. PAGE 104: Bare-faced sandwiches, art-directed by Domino, toasted by Top Banana, and guided by India. PAGE 105: Banger wondering when the orange-and-pomegranate salad will be served. He's been kept waiting long enough.

KALIK

ABOVE AND OPPOSITE: When my mother turned ninety, we set up the tent, spread out the zebra, and had fun glue-gunning 90s onto cardboard hearts. Each napkin was tied in checked ribbon with a feather and a sprig of thyme or a thistle. FOLLOWING PAGES, LEFT: Baby's breath, as I know it, perhaps you know it as gypsophila, has been a longtime favorite. It dries well and can then last a lifetime. FOLLOWING PAGES, RIGHT: 100% cotton fish napkins, perforated on a roll and torn off as needed. Wrinkle free and ready at a moment's notice.

90

JERSEY COW MILK, HIMALAYAN ROCK SALT AND
CULTURED
HAND
UK
ON 022
EC

MACKEREL PÂTÉ

Serves 6

Ingredients

8 oz. (226 g) cream cheese

2–3 smoked mackerel fillets, skinned (approximately 10.5 oz. or 300 g)

1 tsp. horseradish sauce

Juice of half a lemon

Freshly ground black pepper

Directions

1. Place all ingredients into a food processor fitted with a metal blade and blend until smooth.
2. Taste and add more horseradish sauce, lemon juice, and pepper as needed.
3. Serve with freshly toasted crusty bread.

OPPOSITE: I know who made the pâté. I even met the man who made the butter. That's the beauty of eating local. I probably met the cows, too.

A TABLE FOR TWO

And knowing when it's ready

All of my cooking skills have been inherited from my mother, and she can barely boil an egg. (Although she is very good at peeling grapes.)

She once tried to make my father supper. She found a can of spaghetti and read the directions, which clearly said, "Place contents in boiling water." So she did just that: she placed the can in boiling water. The directions never suggested she needed to open the can first. Sometime later, as she sat on the sofa in the drawing room quietly reading, there was a loud explosion from the kitchen as the can in boiling water burst open. My mother rushed into the kitchen, only to find the entire contents had flown out and the spaghetti had shot up and stuck to the ceiling. "Well, at least we know it's ready," she said.

Designer and cook Nathan Turner has patiently tried to teach me how to make a quick, light gnocchi dish for lunch. He made it look so simple that I think I am ready to tackle the recipe alone without his instruction. I just need to remember what sage looks like and how to turn on the oven.

Sometimes it's just easier to order in.

OPPOSITE: A table for two, or even three.

ABOVE: Two vast water bottles, because that's what's needed on a tropical summer's lunch table. OPPOSITE: Veggie rolls and kale salad. Ordered in. FOLLOWING PAGES: I can, however, lay an imaginative table. On this occasion, I used our duvet cover as a tablecloth. Top Banana baked the tart, obviously. Apparently, asparagus is known to contain all sorts of good things that somehow naturally lift your spirits, and my goodness, we can all do with some spirit lifting sometimes.

ABOVE AND OPPOSITE: Armfuls of blossoms and lilacs gathered from the lanes around my mother's home.

NATIVE FLAIR

Bring in the local-ness

My grandparents were always entertaining, as were my parents, as am I. It must be in our blood. I always enjoy our parties. I have fun setting the table in various ways, moving locations, and thinking up new decorations. Whether a simple supper, lively lunch, or formal black-tie gala, every celebration should always feel, in my opinion, like a family affair. I recruit as many of my children as I can to help, however they can, both in the setting up and, I am afraid, the taking down. Or even just covering a cake in roses.

One trick I've picked up over the years is to incorporate something specific from my surroundings to give the occasion a native flair. At home in the Bahamas, for example, it's a table sprinkled with lucky nuts we have collected from the beach or towering vases with palm fronds or a simple assortment of shells mixed with votive candles. When I'm in England, it's small posies of English roses or setting the dinnerware I inherited from my mother, given to her on her wedding day. Of course, there are tears when a side plate or saucer has met an untimely end, and what was once a handsome complete collection is then reduced to a few orphans.

OPPOSITE: The roses are real. The cake is fake. It comes from a box. I held the wibbly-wobbly pieces together with jam and butter icing and long kebab sticks for insurance. FOLLOWING PAGES, LEFT: Glass milk bottles hold up purple agapanthus and complement the plates that I had laid on the table. My mother nearly fainted when she came for lunch and saw I was using them. Apparently, they are eighteenth-century Meissen, meant to be in a museum and not for cookies and ice cream. FOLLOWING PAGES, RIGHT: My first attempt at a naked cake. It felt a bit too naked, so for modesty's sake I sprinkled on some wildflowers. PAGES 124-125: More flowers from our English garden to complement English pea soup.

SALMON EN CROUT

Serves 6

Ingredients

8 tbsp. (113 g) unsalted butter, softened
4 knobs of stem ginger in syrup, finely chopped
3 tbsp. currants
Zest of 1 lemon, finely grated, plus a couple of squeezes of juice
1 shallot, peeled and finely chopped
Sea salt and black pepper
1¾ lbs. (800 g) skinned salmon fillet (preferably in 1 piece)
1 lb. puff-pastry dough (homemade or store-bought)
1 egg, beaten with 1 tsp. water

Directions

1. Preheat oven to 390°F (200°C). Combine the butter, ginger, currants, lemon zest and juice, and shallot in a bowl. Season with salt and pepper.
2. Cut the salmon in half horizontally and season both sides with salt and pepper.
3. Spread half of the butter mixture on one piece of salmon and place the other piece of salmon on top of it.
4. Spread the remaining butter mixture on top of the second piece of salmon.
5. Roll out the puff-pastry dough and place the salmon butter-side down in the middle of the pastry.
6. Bring the sides of the dough together so that they just overlap in the middle of the salmon and seal using the egg wash.
7. Turn over the parcel, seal each end with the egg wash, and trim off any excess dough. Use any leftover dough to decorate the top of the dish. (If you don't have any dough left, score the top to resemble the scales of a fish, but take care not to puncture the dough.)
8. Brush the dough all over with the egg wash and place on a lightly oiled baking sheet. Bake for about 30 minutes, or until the pastry is golden.

LEFT: Those little black bits could easily be mistaken for dead flies. Rest assured: they are currants, not flies.

ABOVE: A tin tub masquerading as a swimming pool for roses.

ABOVE: English summer lunches are always held under threat of rain, so we set this table in the shade of our oak tree hoping it would also act as an umbrella. Possibly more interesting are the roses and peonies arranged in teacups on saucers down the middle of the table.

TEA TIME & PICNICS

AFTERNOON TEA

And other perils

My parents once invited the king of Tonga for afternoon tea. He was exceptionally large, and their London house was quite small. Going down the narrow entrance hallway, he had to turn sideways in order for his vast belly to be accommodated. My mother had bought a substantial chocolate cake from Fortnum & Mason for the occasion. She cut a slice of the cake and offered it to His Majesty, who, without batting an eyelid, took the entire cake, leaving only the tiny slice behind.

Afternoon tea, cream tea, high tea. It can be confusing. Afternoon tea brings the expectation of at least a biscuit or two even if the cake's been eaten by a king, with a cup, saucer, teapot, and cozy. Cream tea means you can expect scones with clotted cream; if there's no clotted cream, then it's a fake. And high tea is something else altogether. It normally involves something hot, like spaghetti hoops on toast, and tends to happen in the early evening; during my childhood, it took place hidden away in a nursery with a nanny.

Teatime is also a time for trivial conversation or polite pleasantries—or not-so-polite ones. I had been invited to speak at an event in North Carolina. They thought because I was English, it would be fun to serve tea for the audience before I spoke. I was seated at a table with several of the committee ladies. A more elderly one leaned across to her neighbor and whispered loudly, "Who is this India Hicks?" There was an awkward silence. I turned to my own neighbor and said, "Oh, dear, I do hope she's not too disappointed." "Well, we were expecting Martha Stewart," my neighbor told me, just as the lights went down and the podium lit up.

It reminded me of the time my grandfather was invited to tea with a grand English hostess and seated next to a young chap who only seemed interested in motorcycles. After tea, the hostess called my grandfather over to see if he had been amused by his companion, and my grandfather confessed, "Not much." "Oh, my dear boy," continued the hostess. "How unfortunate, because that was Lawrence of Arabia."

OPPOSITE: This is a tea tent. We erected it in my mother's garden when more than fifty accomplished American women who I worked with came to explore a proper English tea. It was proper in that it was drizzling with rain, and there were Victoria sponge cake, cucumber sandwiches, and cream scones; it was not proper in that there were jars of licorice allsorts and dolly mixtures—that's not proper at all. That's just mad.

ABOVE: As a child, every afternoon before teatime I was made to go for a brisk walk. "Brush the cobwebs off you," Nanny would say. The idea that one fine day the future might hold such dreams as afternoons in front of a screen playing Candy Crush whilst your mother worked in an office, with no nanny in sight, would have been too much to contemplate. Domino, you have no idea what you get away with.

ABOVE: Everything here was admired on the table and later used in the kitchen.

OPPOSITE: I can't say I made my Bahamian friend Lulu's wedding cake. I only decorated it, with fresh frangipani and a sea glass–green cream icing. Unlike Lulu, who actually made her own wedding dress and designed her husband's white suit, which had a scarlet sash and gold epaulets and even a few made-up medals on his chest for good measure. ABOVE: The coffee cups carry the Prince of Wales's heraldic badge, consisting of three ostrich feathers emerging from a gold coronet. And it shows how much thought this godfather puts into his gifts, long after the godchild deserves them.

THIS BUNNY IS TIRED

Plus broken limbs and Pimm's

"I don't really believe in the Easter Bunny anymore," said Domino a while ago. "Phew, no more Easter egg hunts, this bunny is tired," I replied. I was not in the least mourning the loss of my last child's innocence. I was delighted in not having to hide any more eggs. After twenty years, this bunny was ready for retirement—or not. "Oh, no, we still have to have a hunt," Domino said. "In fact, I was thinking maybe this year Conrad and I can have a hunt before the hunt."

So for the twentieth year in a row, we invited friends, family, and our little local community school to join us in racing across the sandy garden in search of squished chocolate and rabbit ears. We used to serve tea for the parents who waited patiently for their sugar-crazed kids to return. Only a few years ago did we realize it's a much less exhausting exercise when bull-shots, Bloody Marys, and Pimm's are served.

Occasionally in the Bahamas, teatime slips into Pimm's time, even when bunnies aren't involved. It was a weekend, and no one had to rush back to a job. The kids were messing around in the pool, and Captain Bob and his wife, my sweet friend Linda, were telling stories around the table. Their son Joshua appeared whimpering, with our son Amory helping to hold his arm. Hearts sank. During some rough-and-tumble, Joshua's arm had gotten twisted. Badly. Everyone inspected it. The kid stopped crying. Tea continued. It's hard to interrupt tea and Pimm's and stories. The next day, Linda called to say thank you, and what a fun afternoon it had been aside from Joshua's episode. She was just going to nip over to Nassau for a doctor to have a look at the arm to make sure all was OK. A few hours later, she called back. They were in the hospital, and the arm was in a cast. It had actually been broken.

OPPOSITE: The Easter Bunny taking tea. Note the tea strainer, the Twiglets, the cucumber sandwiches with an exotic touch of cream cheese and Marmite, and the sponge cake with a very incorrect cake knife. It's not even a cake knife—it's for carving beef. Standards are slipping again. FOLLOWING PAGES, LEFT: Fruit knives and forks. Truly, that's what they are. They are mother-of-pearl fruit knives and forks with my great-grandfather's initials inlaid in gold. They are never to be used at teatime. They are for fruit served after the dessert at lunchtime. Do not make the mistake of using them at any other time in any other way. FOLLOWING PAGES, RIGHT: Homemade micro meringues sometimes make a teatime appearance.

TEA IS SERVED

Warm the pot first

My mother was recovering from a nasty bout of pneumonia, slowly and in her own stylish way. "Yesterday I got dressed," she told me. "Today I got dressed and put on lipstick." "The hairdresser called to see if I was dead," she continued. She had not missed a hairdressing appointment since 1963. She also never misses tea. Every afternoon at 4 p.m., my mother has tea.

There is a process to it. The teapot needs to be warmed through first before the hot water is added, and she can tell when you skip this step. Always tea leaves, not tea bags. The leaves are strained by her small tea strainer. She even strains the leaves for her dachshund. "No one wants tea leaves in their tea," she would say, placing the saucer of tea on the floor for the dog. Milk, cold, is poured in after—never first. Milk in first reveals an awful lot apparently. There is a tray that fits the teapot, the tea cozy, the tea strainer, the cup, the saucer, the teaspoon. The ivory-handled tea knife, the plate with the hot crumpet and the small starched tea napkin, which must not be confused with the breakfast napkin or the lunch and dinner napkin. They are quite a different size. These all also fit perfectly into place on the tea tray, which is layered with one of her tray cloths, embroidered with her grandfather's initials.

Sometimes we risk going out for tea. The Dorchester tearoom was considered slightly suspect at first, with fussy, fashion-inspired tea cakes. Olivia joined us there. Olivia used to be our head of design when my lifestyle brand was still running. She is French and terribly chic, so it all felt very fitting to be enjoying Prêt-à-Portea. (Don't let that little clever pun slip by you.) Olivia enjoyed herself until my mother began telling some family stories, which ended with one about an uncle on my father's side who died at only a few months old when a wasp flew into his throat. Poor Olivia, I could see her eyes widening in horror. I tried to divert the storytelling by offering her a praline croquant.

OPPOSITE: The tea setup, complete with tea strainer for dog and human and chuckleberry jam. Apparently, the chuckleberry is fast becoming the berry of the moment. Ah, the avant-garde world of jam making.

CHOCOLATE BROWNIES WITH FRESH RASPBERRIES

Serves 16

Ingredients

10 tbsp. (140 g) unsalted butter, softened
1 cup (200 g) chopped dark chocolate
1 cup (225 g) granulated sugar
2 tsp. vanilla extract
Salt
2 large eggs, at room temperature
1 large egg yolk, at room temperature
⅔ cup (85 g) all-purpose flour
1½ cups (187 g) fresh raspberries

Directions

1. Preheat oven to 350°F (180°C). Line an 8-inch square tin with silicone or parchment paper.
2. In a double boiler or a bowl set over a pan of simmering water, melt the butter and the chocolate together. Remove pan or bowl from the heat and let cool slightly.
3. Whisk the sugar, vanilla extract, and a pinch of salt into the chocolate mixture. It will seem a bit grainy, and that's OK. Then whisk in the eggs and egg yolk until well mixed.
4. Sift in the flour and mix for about a minute until batter is thick and smooth. Then fold in the fresh raspberries and pour the batter into the prepared tin.
5. Bake for 35 to 45 minutes, or until a knife inserted in the middle comes out with only moist crumbs clinging to it.
6. Remove the brownies from the oven and place a damp tea towel over the tin to keep the top from becoming crispy. (If you like a crispy top, leave the towel off.) Allow brownies to cool completely and then cut into squares.

OPPOSITE: Abandoned on a desert island, what would your desire be? Mine is hot buttered toast and Top Banana's chocolate raspberry brownies, obviously.

Nestlé
After Eight
MINT CHOCOLATE THINS

PICNICKING

The proper way

As a small child, I asked my father to write in my little autograph book. In his distinctive hand, he left the phrase *Good taste and design are by no means dependent upon money.* I had no idea what that meant. Always the discerning tastemaker, aged eight years old David Hicks called the local tailor to his parents' house and commissioned a dinner jacket. The only problem was, he had nowhere to wear the little dinner jacket.

He was truly an individual. A room with too many small objects was considered restless, and bright blue swimming pools were vulgar. (Ours was painted black.) He ran over the daffodils that grew outside his library window because they were the wrong shade of yellow. He would rearrange the furniture in the guest room of the surprised friends he was staying with. And he was never, ever afraid to speak his mind. "I loathe the color used on modern buildings. Red dogs are hideous. I hate satin, I hate wrought iron, and I hate picnics."

My mother, on the other hand, loved them—picnics, that is. We enjoyed a great deal of time holidaying in the summer between Ireland and Scotland. Not with my father, obviously, but with my aunt, uncle, and a herd of cousins. An inordinate amount of time was spent on the edges of rivers, whisking away mosquitoes, in drizzling rain waiting for a salmon to bite. We would each have made up our own little picnic to sustain us through the day, often wrapped in a tea towel and ever so slightly tasting of peat.

OPPOSITE: Stainless steel mugs, wooden knives and forks, glass water bottle, recycled veggie pita box, compostable craft napkins, and an inherited picnic basket. Are we ticking all the sustainable boxes? FOLLOWING PAGES, LEFT: Arranging fresh figs, prosciutto, Gorgonzola, and raw spinach on a wooden board is something else I can cook. FOLLOWING PAGES, RIGHT: It appears here that we only packed Orangina in the basket, but cushions and a sun hat are nearly as essential.

OPPOSITE: My father built a house in the Bahamas by mixing sand from the beach with a rough cement. Just after it was completed, he decided sand was an annoyance and got into everything. He never returned to his house of sand. But the rest of the family did, and we found ways to avoid sandy sandwiches on beach picnics by bringing a folding table and stools. ABOVE: On other occasions, we create a makeshift table from old pallets that are used for shipping goods to the island. After the picnic, you can dig a pit and use the pallets to start an impressive fire.

G&CO

HONEY MUSTARD SAUSAGES

Serves 6

Ingredients

1 lb. (454 g) British bangers (or any pork sausages)

3 tbsp. grainy mustard

2 tbsp. runny honey

Directions

1. Preheat the oven to 375°F (190°C).
2. Place the sausages in an ovenproof dish and bake 30 minutes until browned.
3. Mix the mustard and honey together in a bowl.
4. Remove the sausages from the oven and cut them into bite-size pieces, leaving them in the dish.
5. Pour the mustard-honey mixture over the sausages and put the pan back in the oven to cook another 10 minutes until the mixture has gone lovely and gooey.

PREVIOUS PAGES, LEFT: Scenes from picnicking on David's slipper launch one summer afternoon and later during the Henley Royal Regatta. Which explains why Amory is dressed in a suit looking very James Bond. PREVIOUS PAGES, RIGHT: I can't cook anything sensible that would sustain a human being, but I can bake a cake, especially when using different-sized tins and lots of cream and fruit. OPPOSITE: Our picnic basket followed us out to the Bahamas from England, updated slightly with bamboo knives and forks. Beware of After Eights on a tropical beach. FOLLOWING PAGES: The ploughman's lunch is typically wrapped in a tea towel and also traditionally involves Granny Smith apples, chunky bread, eggs, Branston pickle, and disgusting real pickles that make your breath stink for a long time afterward.

BIRTHDAY CAKE & CHRISTMAS CRACKERS

WISDOM AND DISCRETION

On the celebration of birthdays

My mother and I were discussing my fiftieth birthday. I had hoped for advice on a new era, but what I heard was a small warning: "Darling, you should now have reached the age of wisdom and discretion." She then said with precision, "Impulse should be a thing of the past." Perhaps best not to share with her that last summer I had, on impulse, bungee jumped off the bridge at Victoria Falls in Zimbabwe. One hundred and eleven meters high. A four-second free fall as a celebration of the benchmark birthday. I also neglected to mention celebrating the same birthday during an evening in New York, on a hotel rooftop, with many friends and colleagues. Again, on impulse, I pulled down all the pretty helium balloons, sucked out the air, and gave the expected toast in a ridiculous Mickey Mouse voice.

Whether you are five or fifty-five, I do believe birthdays should be celebrated with happiness and a large dose of fun. Although that's not always the case. Do you remember Chuckie from the *Rugrats*, red hair, oversize specs, best friend of Tommy Pickles? Felix was a fan, and for one of his early birthdays, we organized for a Chuckie look-alike to come to Harbour Island. Rather surprisingly, we had discovered you could hire a six-foot-tall Chuckie in Nassau (back then, it was hard to find smoked salmon in Nassau, let alone a six-foot-tall Chuckie). He arrived off the ferry, very hot and sweaty, carrying his head in his arms. Felix and Wesley were chasing birthday balloons around the garden when Chuckie got to the house. Felix took one look at this gigantic cartoon character and ran in fright to the bathroom, where he stayed for the rest of the party.

Felix's eighteenth birthday was more successful. Eighteen friends to celebrate eighteen years around long trestle tables under the stars, lit by candlelight. There were very few flowers blooming, so David covered the table with two gigantic palm fronds on top of the white tablecloths, anchored by two locally grown bunches of bananas in the center, with piles of pineapples, watermelons, and oranges spilling off in each direction and dozens of tea lights dotted between shells in and among the fruit. With this mass of different tropical fruits, it looked sensational, but I don't think the partygoers even noticed. The last thing on the minds of 18 eighteen-year-olds is fruit.

OPPOSITE: About to unwisely give a helium toast.

ABOVE: Felix and Wesley, arms around each other for most of their lives.

ABOVE: Royal icing tongue and marshmallow teeth. FOLLOWING PAGES, LEFT: A sparkling range that includes Wesley's eighteen cupcakes, a domino cake for Domino, a ConRAT cake for Conrad, and a "Holy Crap" cake with little shits around the outside for Amory, who, for the record, is not a little shit. FOLLOWING PAGES, RIGHT: Exploding Malteser cake; a droopy candle on my own cake that summed up how I felt that year—it had been a hard one; rainbow cupcakes; and eight, for a very accessorized 8 year-old.

Happy
Congrats
Birthday

HOLY
CRAP

18

HAPPY BIRTHDAY

SPONGE CAKE

Serves 8

Ingredients

16 tbsp. (126 g) margarine, softened
1 cup caster sugar (or superfine sugar)
4 eggs, lightly beaten
1½ cups plus 2 tbsp. self-rising flour, sifted
1–2 tbsp. milk, any type

Directions

1. Preheat oven to 350°F (180°C). Grease and flour two 8-inch round cake tins (or line with greaseproof paper).
2. Cream the margarine and sugar together until light and fluffy.
3. Gradually add the beaten eggs a bit at a time. If it looks as if the mixture is curdling, add a tablespoon of flour.
4. Fold in the sifted flour. If the mixture seems too heavy, add a little bit of milk. Then divide batter equally between the two cake tins.
5. Bake in the middle of the oven for about 20 minutes, or until a toothpick comes out clean.
6. Remove cakes from the oven and run a knife around the edge of each. Turn out onto a wire rack to cool.
7. Add icing of your choice, the most important step.

OPPOSITE: Hugs and homemade cakes.

ABOVE AND OPPOSITE: At least a decade between these two images of Amory. The blowing of candles should never get old.

ABOVE: Rissy, who's looked after us forever, in the Hibiscus Hill headquarters. OPPOSITE: The joy of having your brothers at your birthday. FOLLOWING PAGES: A matrix of birthday parties, cakes, and games through the years. Do note the pineapple palm tree—that took a lot of architectural precision.

Conrad
Happy Birthday

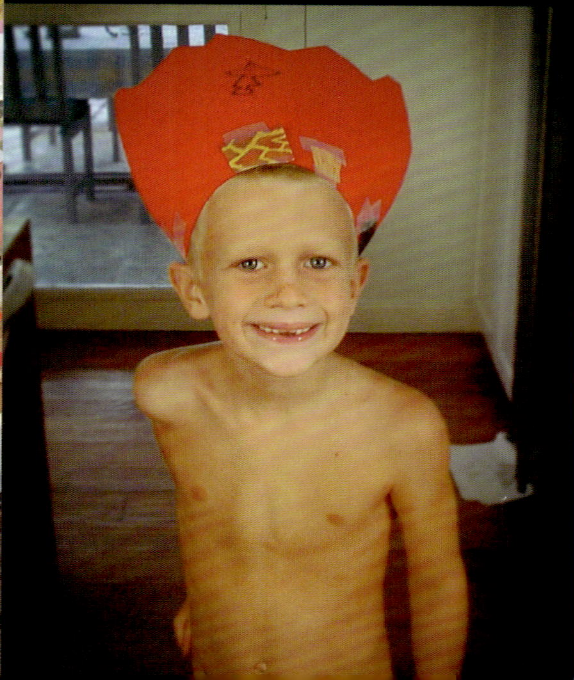

EMORY

THE
BEATLES

FIND A THEME

And buy a glue gun

It was my longtime friend Linda's birthday. We had invited some friends to pop in for a drink in the garden of the Sugar Mill, the boutique we founded together. We decided to open a bottle of champagne early, you know, just to test it before everyone arrived. After a few glasses, we suddenly had the brilliant booze-induced idea that the garden needed sprucing up. We had handfuls of Indian saris that at one confused time we thought would sell well. We covered chairs and cushions, and draped candleholders from the tree with stretches of the fabric, then put on some Bollywood music and opened more champagne. The birthday was transformed.

Domino's eleventh birthday was trickier. Ten had been easy—it was unicorns, obviously unicorns. But eleven was like, What the heck do we do? So I returned to a theme: rose gold. Once chosen, you'll discover your theme everywhere. We even found a rose-gold karaoke microphone and rose-gold flared candles.

I found inexpensive paper poufs in a mix of dusty pinks. They were inexpensive, I later discovered, because we had to pouf them ourselves and that took hours. I ordered a length of raw pink netting, which I chopped with kitchen scissors and then staple-gunned to the layer of plywood we had to cover the nice wooden table underneath. The stapling looked so shit that I then staple-gunned some greenery I had left over from a flower display over the top. Final touches were rose gold–foiled paper cups, rose-gold mason jars with twinkly lights, folding bamboo chairs without cushions (I cared much less about the comfort of the eleven-year-old bottoms than I did about my white cushions), and cheap star string lights.

The recipe for a successful eleven-year-old birthday party seemed to be a mix of the above with the additional ingredients of a wrought-iron tub filled with water to bob for apples followed by a head dunk in flour hunting for a cork, which produced huge amounts of giggles and revolting gluey faces; there was also stamping on balloons tied to your ankles, a chocolate fountain, and a good amount of musical statues. But really, from a decoration point of view, the only ingredient you will ever need is a glue gun.

OPPOSITE: Bollywood at its best in the Bahamas.

ABOVE: We created a circular frame from which we hung lights and paper poufs. On the table I placed a stand I use for flower arrangements when I am feeling Martha Stewart-y. I glue-gunned more poufs onto this and then added real greenery and hydrangeas. OPPOSITE: Dusty-pink bear feet, rose gold–dipped feathers, sprinkles, cupcakes, and candles. It took most of the day for me to put this together—a mistake I did not make the next year, when we had hot dogs on the grass and a water-balloon fight that took about fifteen minutes to set up.

DOMINO

ABOVE: It's important to have your sorbet match your theme.

ABOVE: Color is everything.

HOT AND COLD CHRISTMAS

And our weird traditions

Our Christmas in the tropics might be a blend of two strong cultures, but it's consistent in its traditions. Our tree is a real fir that travels by boat and is very thirsty by the time it finally settles in our Bahamian sitting room. We decorate it together as a family. There are quite a few arguments about the balance of the lights, the placement of the ornaments, and who will put the fairy on the top. We have collected over the years Mr. and Mrs. Claus from Haiti, a red double-decker bus from London, a weird little rainbow fish, and a sugar cookie in the shape of a star made by one of the teenage boys when he was tiny. It's terrifically stale now, but every year it reappears on a branch of the tree.

On Christmas Eve, we gather around the fireplace, which we light even if it's boiling hot, just so we feel English-y and Christmassy. We hang the stockings, which were made for each of my children by my mother's dressmaker, with their names stitched on in bold lettering. At 10 p.m., David and I go to midnight mass. Yes, you read that correctly: ten o'clock is midnight mass. Rissy, who has been part of our family since we moved to the island, sings in the choir or hands out the service sheets. Either way, it's an important role and we go to support her, although I hope God notices, too.

After church, David and I stuff the stockings. It's always late, I'm always overtired, bits of tape peel off, and presents get muddled up, but I'm also excited for the morning. I love Christmas.

OPPOSITE: We always use the ceramic plates David gave me for our Christmas lunch; they have charming Christmas trees painted on them, in case you had not noticed. FOLLOWING PAGES, LEFT: One year, in a last-minute rush, I put a plastic green garland down the table. Sounds horrible, doesn't it? But I think in the dark, lit only by candles, we just about got away with it. FOLLOWING PAGES, RIGHT: Bond and Domino have grown considerably. The stockings have remained the same size, thankfully, as Father Christmas is already rather daunted by them.

ABOVE AND OPPOSITE: Our Christmas table. I realized recently just how many bizarre Christmas customs we Brits have. Christmas crackers, for example, are not something you eat with cheese. They are made from paper, have a loud bang when pulled, and are filled with paper crowns, silly jokes, and small toys. FOLLOWING PAGES: My father made all the design decisions when I was growing up; the only time my mother was allowed to get creative was in the wrapping of our presents. I take this as seriously as she did.

Merry Christmas

MERRY CHRISTMAS TO YOU!

For you

Merry
For you

CHRISTMAS
AMORY
LOVE FROM MUMMY & DADDY
WESLEY
FELIX
CONRAD
LOVE FROM MUMMY & DADDY
CHRISTMAS
CONRAD

ABOVE: The greatest present I am given every year is the gift of Claire, our Top Banana, as she cooks the turkey and all the traditional trimmings that go with it.

ABOVE: Each holiday I change up our table a little—dried fruit and palm fronds one year, bowls filled with oranges the next. Or branches of fir and pine cones, with blue-and-white ceramics and tartan napkins, as shown here.

LIGHTING THE PLUM PUDDING

Year after year after year

As a child, I was always a little confused as to why the Father Christmas I met on Christmas Eve always smelled faintly of milk. He was, of course, the milkman on my grandfather's estate. Mind you, this is not as confusing as my children growing up in the Bahamas, with a black Father Christmas, only to discover elsewhere in the world there were white imposters scattered about the place.

Domino will be up first. She will wake her brothers, thrilled that Father Christmas found us. Five kids, two cats, a few dogs, and the stockings pile onto our bed and the chaos begins. We always have Christmas crackers, and we always wear the paper hats, blow the plastic whistles, and tell the silly jokes. We also always set the plum pudding on fire—we can never find the matches to light it, and we always have too much brandy in the brandy butter.

We try most years to slip away at some point to the churchyard to say a quick hello to Wesley's mama, buried peacefully there. We don't want her to be alone. And before the day ends, I will call my own mama, in England, who will be with my brother and sister and their families. I miss them. A lot. But I am thankful for the love of our own family and the friends gathered with us celebrating Christmas in the Bahamas.

PREVIOUS PAGES: As seen here, year after year after year, we set our plum puddings alight, with a lot of brandy, matches, and burnt fingers. It's a tradition. OPPOSITE: Where I can, I like to use decorations that have a strong natural fragrance on the tabletop, especially during the holidays. Fir and pine cones are there at Christmas; mint and eucalyptus covered the tables for New Year's Eve.

A NEW DECADE

And hope for the future

It was a natural disaster and a national crisis. Hurricane Dorian had brought utter ruin to the islands of Grand Bahama and Abaco. It was not just the power of the winds but the surge of water that followed. A tsunami wave had raced toward these islands and angrily swept away hundreds of people who will never be accounted for. Thousands of others were left completely homeless. We live on an island only seventy miles away. It could have been us. So, on New Year's Eve, with help from generous friends in our small community, we hosted a party for a few hundred people to raise desperately needed funds for the Global Empowerment Mission, a responsible, smart, hands-on foundation that is helping to rebuild lives.

Claire went into Top Banana mode. She borrowed industrial-sized saucepans in which she cooked soups, was lent fridge space around the island to store salmon, ordered in exotic vegetables, sourced out crusty breads, and peeled sackfuls of potatoes as delicious sweet hams bubbled in Coca-Cola on stove tops for hours on end, always her pièce de résistance. Crates of chilled champagne and cases of wine began to arrive. Wheels of cheese and baskets of fruit were delivered. A crew from the Other Side, a family-run hotel, rescued us with tents, tables, goodwill, and manpower. But there was plenty of womanpower too, hanging chandeliers, hoisting lighting, and stringing up branches from tropical trees. Napkins came from Pomegranate and linens from Penny Morrison; piles of mint, roses, and eucalyptus were given by the Prince of Dunmore. Bars were set up, countless candles were lit, and the band rehearsed whilst I tore out my hair over the seating plan. So many politics were involved in that.

The music started, the ice clinked, and guests swarmed on the terrace and down the drive as children spilled out across the grass. Drinks drifted into dinner; Captain Bob said an opening prayer reminding us why we had come together. Fireworks were let off into the inky sky. We danced, laughed, and lingered as we welcomed in a new decade together, hopeful for our neighbors' future thanks to the many generous donations made that night.

OPPOSITE AND FOLLOWING PAGES: Every table was named after one of the settlements hit by the hurricane. During dinner, we asked our friend Henry St. George to speak about Grand Bahama, where he lives. He spoke quietly and eloquently about the progress that had been made, but reminded us there was so much more work to be done.

Grand Bahama

THE GREAT BRITISH BREAKFAST

BREAKFAST IN BED

The professional way

Every morning, a breakfast tray is brought into my mother's room. It's a proper tray with legs, so it stands correctly. The breakfast itself will have been decided the night before, and it can range from a boiled egg to fish cakes to half a grapefruit. There is always toast regardless, with the crusts cut off and placed in the toast rack. There is a tiny china dish that holds the honey and the butter; the dish is divided because you would not want your honey running into the butter. My mother has always been impeccably dressed, and breakfast is no exception. Without fail, she will wear a bed jacket, and there is a selection of them: lighter for summer, warmer for winter. My mother reminds us all that breakfast is the most important meal of the day. And she is a professional.

Sometimes I am invited to give a talk at a design show. I usually include a picture of my mother's breakfast tray. It's always very popular. I talk a little about her upbringing and the extraordinary homes she spent her childhood in. I once also told the story of my grandmother, who left my mother and aunt in Hungary, thinking they would be safe with their nanny and governess as she went on her merry way exploring Europe. But then she discovered that she could not remember where she had left the children, and it took her six months to retrace her footsteps and find them. Two young mothers in the front row of that talk had their mouths wide open as they listened. Afterward, they came up to me. "Oh no," I said. "Were you very shocked by that?" "Not at all," they replied. "We were trying to work out where we could drop off our children for six months."

I will often sit beside my mother on her bed whilst she has breakfast and we chat. She has an encyclopedic mind and is fascinating as a result. When my business was up and running, I would join conference calls with the office in L.A. from my mother's bed. It was nighttime in L.A. and breakfast time in Oxfordshire. I once jumped on a video link to join the CEO and several lawyers. Just as we were starting this important call, my mother appeared in her nightie from the bathroom. "Have you borrowed my hairbrush?" she asked. I desperately tried to find the mute button on my computer as she continued, "You really are an annoying child."

OPPOSITE: This picture is actually a cheat. This is not morning breakfast in bed at all. It's tea on a tray in the afternoon. My mother was recovering from pneumonia, and the doctor had insisted she remain in bed. Chocolate Kit Kats and buttered buns were ideal medicine.

EGGS BENEDICT WITH SMOKED SALMON

Serves 1

Ingredients

1 English muffin

Butter

Baby spinach, fresh or slightly wilted with boiling water and drained

Smoked salmon

Lemon

2 eggs, as fresh as possible

Salt and freshly ground black pepper

Homemade or store-bought hollandaise sauce

Directions

1. Toast the muffin and spread each side with butter.
2. Put a small handful of baby spinach on top of each muffin half. Then place a good serving of smoked salmon on top of the spinach.
3. Squeeze some lemon juice on the salmon.
4. Poach your eggs to however you like them.
5. Place the poached eggs on top of the smoked salmon and season with salt and freshly ground black pepper.
6. Drizzle each egg with as much hollandaise sauce as you like. This can be cold or slightly warmed.

OPPOSITE: That perfect moment just as the egg ruptures. FOLLOWING PAGES, LEFT: Breakfast china. A set of china used only for that specific meal. That is a thing. FOLLOWING PAGES, RIGHT: I once had a colleague and her young daughter come and stay. One morning, the sleepy daughter appeared at the breakfast table. She was looking between my twenty-year-old son and me. “Are you his mother?” she asked. “Yes, but did you think I was his sister?” I said hopefully. “No,” she replied without hesitation. “I thought you were his grandmother.”

CEREAL
KILLER

PATIENCE IS A VIRTUE?

The most important meal of the day

I was at a conference. It had started early. We were served breakfast whilst gathered around tables, looking up at a vast screen. The speaker clicked over to another slide. "Which one are you?" she asked the 500 women in the room pointing at the screen. "Are you the person who enters the elevator and works out if it's safe to get in: How many people? How much weight? Is there a risk involved? Or are you the one who sees entering the elevator as an opportunity to chat to other people, time to perhaps even make an introduction? Or are you the one who just wants to get to the floor you need to get to as quickly as possible with no interruption?"

She paused as the audience worked out who they were. "Of course," she continued, "There is another person, one that pushes the Close Door button impatiently and repeatedly, over and over—but I have not listed that person . . . ."

I looked down at my granola. That person sounded very familiar. That endlessly impatient person who could not wait for an egg to poach or toast to brown. Who would not even take the time to sit down to breakfast, let alone lie in bed to have it. Except when the kids are home on holiday. Then I take breakfast seriously, as it's the only meal where I can catch up with them nearly one on one. Lunch I'll be back in my office and they will have escaped with friends and when we are reunited at supper there are too many voices talking at once.

Domino, being the youngest, will wake first. She will spread Marmite on her toast and together we might color or paint at the table, before she wanders off again. Conrad follows. He'll eat cereal, then pancakes, then eggs with bacon, then toast and Marmite, and then possibly have another bowl of cereal before he leaves to start his day. The older three boys meander down together, more Marmite is spread, more eggs are scrambled, a lot more bacon is eaten. Everyone is civilized. Everyone talks nicely to their mother. Breakfast really is the most important meal of the day.

OPPOSITE: This spoon is perfectly suited to our breakfast table. FOLLOWING PAGES: At first I was a little unsure of the china set we inherited with the house we bought in the Bahamas, being a color and pattern I would not naturally have chosen. But now, twenty-five years later, they are part of the fabric of our family life, although admittedly so many of the tea- and coffee cups have been broken over the years that we now have to drink from the double-handled soup bowls.

MARMITE

BIG SQUEEZE
YEAST EXTRACT

COCOA PEBBLES

ROSTED
FLAKES
Nutrition at a Glance
THEY'RE GR-R-REAT!
HONEY SMACKS
fuel up for action!
MARMITE
YEAST EXTRACT

FLINT WOOD
YEAST EXTRACT
RICH IN B VITAMINS • 100% VEGETARI

OPPOSITE: Marmite, you either love it or hate it. Clearly most of us love it. We've even had it personalized. Jenga, our parrot, however, did not love it. He loved biting our toes. Which explains why Wesley's feet are on the chair. Well, I hope that's the explanation. ABOVE: Our attempt at a breakfast tray for my mother in the days when she would stay with us. The dachshund eggcup was a great success, and the tray without legs was politely never commented on.

PORRIDGE

Serves 1

Ingredients

½ cup (50 g) rolled porridge oats

1½ cups (350 ml) milk

Salt

Toppings

Directions

1. Put the oats, milk, and a pinch of salt into a heavy bottomed saucepan.
2. Stir with a wooden spoon.
3. Bring to a steady simmer for about 5–6 mins. Stir it as often as you can. This will help to stop it from burning and also give you smooth, creamy porridge.
4. If you like a runnier porridge add a bit more liquid.
5. Put into a bowl and add your favorite topping.

OPPOSITE: As children we were always told, watch your grandfather . . . and don't copy him. He would be dipping his spoon into the honey pot, then holding it at a great height and letting it dangerously dribble down into his porridge. FOLLOWING PAGE, LEFT: Outside the pantry, my mother's cupboards are brimming with assorted china sets. They all have a different purpose, apparently. This is a breakfast coffee set; you can tell by the size of the cup. Understanding which size coffee cup should be used for which moment of the day is more complicated than attaining a university degree. FOLLOWING PAGE, RIGHT: And this little set is part of the "wake-up coffee" collection. That's the coffee cup that is brought to you before the breakfast tray arrives, when the curtains are first opened. PAGES 218-219: Displayed with panache on plates passed down through the generations. A healthier breakfast message, except if you insist on covering the bananas in cream and brown sugar. Waves lapping, palms swaying, cool grass under bare feet. This is breakfast on a small outer island in the Bahamas, and I never take it for granted.

THE BOSS.

THE END

ACKNOWLEDGMENTS

The thanks go heavily to my other half, David, my harshest but most valued critic, and my mother, who reassured me that even though my brother was planning a fascinating scholarly book on tombs, my fluffy book on cakes and Christmas crackers would also sit on her bookshelf. Thank you to my five children, whom I annoy a lot; Brooke Shields, who was generous with her words and always wider and lower in her splits; Linda Griffin and her stylish eye; and David Loftus, who spent meticulous time making magic happen with food photography. And also to Charles Miers and Rizzoli; Kathleen Jayes, my patient editor; and of course Claire Williams, who by now needs no introduction.

But a large portion of these thanks go to Brittan Goetz, who photographs, art directs, and spends an inordinate amount of time with me on the phone discussing not only content, but also climate change, culture, and our kids.

There comes a time where you realize that everything could just have been a dream and only those things preserved in pictures have any possibility of remaining real, so thank you also to anyone who bought this book, making the grand pleasures of life a reality.

First published in the United States of America in 2020 by
Rizzoli International Publications, Inc.
300 Park Avenue South
New York, NY 10010
www.rizzoliusa.com

Copyright © 2020 India Hicks
Foreword: Brooke Shields
Photography Credits:
India Hicks: 22, 26, 34, 43, 44, 46, 47, 48, 49, 53, 54, 56, 57, 66, 70, 72, 73, 76, 77, 83, 84, 85, 88, 100, 103, 105, 106, 107, 119, 120, 122, 123, 124, 128, 129, 131, 132, 134, 135, 136, 137, 138, 152, 153, 159, 162, 163, 164, 165, 168, 169, 170, 171, 172, 173, 174, 176, 177, 178, 179, 180, 183, 184, 185, 186, 187, 188, 189, 190, 191, 192, 202, 210, 212, 213, 222 **Brittan Goetz:** 10, 13, 16, 17, 18, 19, 20, 22, 24, 25, 28, 29, 30, 32, 36, 38, 39, 40, 41, 49, 52, 53, 58, 60, 61, 62, 64, 65, 68, , 73, 74, 75, 78, 82, 91, 92, 94, 95, 96, 98, 99, 102, 103, 104, 108, 109, 112, 114, 115, 140, 141, 142, 146, 149, 150, 151, 156, 157, 160, 182, 206, 207, 208, 216, 217, 218, 219, 220 **David Loftus**: Pages 14, 50, 80, 86, 105, 110, 116, 117, 125, 126, 144, 154, 201, 204, 214 **Alexandra Mirzyantz**: Page 26, **David Flint Wood**: Page 71, 118, **Claire Williams**: Page 148, **Paola Wells**: Pages 194, 196, 197, 198

Publisher: Charles Miers
Senior Editor: Kathleen Jayes
Design: Brittan Goetz
Production Manager: Barbara Sadick
Managing Editor: Lynn Scrabis

All rights reserved. No part of this publication may be reproduced, stored in a retrieval system, or transmitted in any form or by any means, electronic, mechanical, photocopying, recording, or otherwise, without prior consent of the publishers.

Printed in China

2021 2022 2023 2024 / 10 9 8 7 6 5

ISBN: 978-0-8478- 6889-6
Library of Congress Control Number: 2020937209

Visit us online:
Facebook.com/RizzoliNewYork
Twitter: @Rizzoli_Books
Instagram.com/RizzoliBooks
Pinterest.com/RizzoliBooks
Youtube.com/user/RizzoliNY
Issuu.com/Rizzoli